Target Archery

How to Shoot a Bow and Arrow

An Introduction

By

Samantha Rivera

Target Archery

Copyright © 2017

All rights reserved. This book or any portion thereof may not be reproduced or used in any manner whatsoever without the express written permission of the publisher except for the use of brief quotations in a book review.

ISBN: 9781549994951

Warning and Disclaimer

Every effort has been made to make this book as accurate as possible. However, no warranty or fitness is implied. The information provided is on an "as-is" basis. The author and the publisher shall have no liability or responsibility to any person or entity with respect to any loss or damages that arise from the information in this book.

Publisher Contact

Skinny Bottle Publishing

books@skinnybottle.com

Contents

Introduction to Target Archery 1
Chapter I 3
    The History of Target Archery 3
Chapter II 5
    Getting Started With the Right Tools 5
Chapter III 9
    Understanding Your Compound Bow 9
Chapter IV 11
    Understanding Your Recurve 11
Chapter V 14
    The Target Options for Your Practice 14
Chapter VI 17
    Indoor Target Archery 17
Chapter VII 19
    Outdoor Target Archery 19
Chapter VIII 21
    Competing in Target Archery 21
Chapter IX 24
    Tips and Tricks Your Coach Will Tell You 24
Chapter X 27
    Is Target Archery For You? 27
Conclusion 30

Introduction to Target Archery

Target archery is something everyone can enjoy, no matter how old you are and nearly no matter how young you are. It's super easy for you to learn about and maybe even start experimenting with on your own (or with a club). After all, for a lot of people, starting a new sport can be a great experience and one that they really like to do as much as possible.

So what is target archery? Well, the basic just of target archery is that it's a sport that uses a bow and arrows to shoot, well, a target. There are two different types of bows, namely a recurve and a compound, that you can use for this type of archery. (There are others as well but these are the ones used most frequently for target shooting). You get to choose which of these bows you like best because the experience of shooting each one is going to be slightly different. Of course, we'll get into the differences and why you might choose one or the other later.

Whichever one you choose, you're going to use it for shooting arrows (which you'll also have to pick out a bit later). You may be asking yourself why you should even be trying out target archery and there are a few reasons. Now, number one is that some people enjoy hunting, or going out into the wilderness to kill their own food, but not everyone is a fan. If you're interested in hunting, then target archery can be a good way to practice. If you're not interested in hunting (and not all of us who enjoy target archery are) you can simply use it as a way to have some fun and maybe get a little into the competitive aspect. It's entirely up to you.

Of course, we're getting a little ahead of ourselves now. After all, you don't even really know what you're doing when it comes to target archery yet, so how are you supposed to know if you might want to go hunting or start competing? There's a whole lot to the process, but don't worry, and don't get overwhelmed. It's going to be a whole lot of fun too.

Chapter I

The History of Target Archery

Before you really start getting deep into anything about the sport, you should know how it came about and what it really means for those who practice it. You should know about the first people to use the sport and definitely how it became something that everyone was doing. (Okay, so not everyone is really doing it but a lot of people are. But just how did that happen?

Well, as you can likely imagine, archery has been around for a very long time. Our distant ancestors, the first humans to walk the earth, used hunting as a way to put food on their table. We don't know for certain that they used bows and arrows in the Stone Age, but we believe it to have been a very likely possibility. What we do know is that the ancient Egyptians used bows and arrows to hunt for their food. That was all the way back about 5,000 years ago that people first started building their own bows and arrows to get the food their family needed.

Of course, that's not really when it became a sport, but it is when things started sprawling across the world. Egypt started things off, but China began using a bow and arrows around 1766 BC and then continued spreading it as well, bringing it all the way to Japan by the sixth century. Though the Egyptians had it first, it's believed they really only used archery as a way to hunt or to conduct war and never had competitions about it. They would have been inclined to practice, but not nearly to the extent that we do today (and definitely not just for the purpose of having fun).

The Chinese were the first to actually create a sport out of target archery and conduct tournaments for the nobles. The Japanese continued these types of activities and actually modified one of their martial arts to accommodate shooting with a bow and arrow. Called Kyudo, the Japanese use this to develop physically, mentally and spiritually and archery is considered a part of the process. As time continued on, the Greco-Roman period shows that archery was a sport and a hunting tool at that time even.

People continued to practice and become even better. They also began to see archery as a way to show off their own personal skills. In fact, it was their experience with bows and arrows that allowed Atilla the Hun to conquer much of his territory. It was also bows and arrows that allowed the Turkish people to repel the Crusaders. In short, a lot of things have been done with a bow and arrow that people wouldn't have been able to accomplish before. Who wouldn't want to give it a shot and see what they can do?

Around the world, the activity has been used as a life-saving one for those who need to put food on the table and a fun one for those who wanted to improve their sporting fun. Even those who used it as a way to hunt also started looking at it as an enjoyable experience as well. That's because practicing and competing helped to make each participant even stronger and better at archery. As a result, the sport continued to grow and people continued to get better and better at it as well.

Nowadays there are still a lot of people who use a bow and arrows to hunt for food (though it isn't a requirement anymore). It's not used for warfare, however (at least not in our country or other developed or even developing nations). Instead, archery is considered a sport. Those who use a bow and arrow to hunt do it because they like the experience, not because they have to do it in order to get the food their family needs. Most of those who participate, however, do it simply because they enjoy archery as a pastime. There's no longer any need for anything else. But of course, you have to know about the equipment and everything it takes to be successful if you're going to start, right?

Chapter II

Getting Started With the Right Tools

So just what does it take to be successful when you're practicing archery? Well, it's going to depend a lot on you and it's definitely going to depend on the type of bow you get, but there are plenty of things that you can do to make the experience more fun and less work (unless you want to do it the more traditional way of course). There are all different pieces to the bows that you might use and it's important to understand a little bit about them before you begin.

Quiver: This piece of equipment isn't absolutely necessary, but it's going to make things a whole lot easier for you. That's because a quiver is what holds the arrows that you are going to shoot with. The quiver doesn't have to be anything extra special, though there are all kinds of them out there that you can (and should) try. The oldest quivers would have been made of a simple piece of animal skin that formed one, single space for the arrows to go. Now you can get larger ones that have more than one space for arrows and even pockets that let you carry other things with you too.

A quiver may have a loop on it so it attaches directly to your belt or it may have a clip that lets you attach it to a pocket or the side of your pants instead. No matter what you like best, a quiver is going to be a great tool to have and you can buy them just about anywhere. What's really great is you can get a variety of different price ranges for a quiver too, so you don't have to spend a lot of money to get something that works for you. Just keep in mind what you want to be able to carry.

Release: A release is what you're going to use to pull the string on your bow back and then let it go so the arrow shoots towards the target. This isn't absolutely required either (and we'll talk about the main alternative in a moment) but it can be beneficial. If you're not using a release then you'll be using your fingers to pull the bow string back. While this isn't the traditional way to do things, it is definitely a lot easier on your fingers and that means you can shoot for a lot longer without as much pain.

A release can be quite small because some of them only fit in the palm of your hand. Others are much larger because they have a strap that fits around your wrist and then into the palm of your hand. If you're not sure you'll be able to hold the release at all times or you're afraid you might drop it then one with a wrist strap is a good idea. Either way, the release is going to have a small divot in the front that you push up to the string of the bow. On some you have to flip the lever to close the latch around the string, others you just push the string in far enough and it latches on its own.

Once you've done this you just pull it back slowly and pull slowly on the lever to release the string when you're ready. Some releases are very extravagant and though they may not look much different, they're a whole lot more sensitive than others. These ones are called 'hair triggers' and that means if you so much as tap the lever it will release. If you're hunting or if you're really good with a release you may like these because there's no time for you to move once you've sighted in. If you're a little jumpy (like some of us) you may want a release that requires a slight amount more effort to pull.

Fingers: If you're not going to use a release it's recommended that you at least use 'fingers.' Now, we're not talking about the ones attached to your hands. These fingers are actually a small pad that goes on the inside of your pointer and middle finger (the two you'll use to pull back the string). The pad helps to get a good grip on the string without tearing up your actual fingers. After all, that string is quite abrasive if you keep pulling it back again and again. You want something that will keep you from hurting yourself.

Also, if you tend to sweat at all or if you're in an area where the weather isn't so great you could get moisture on your fingers, and that can mess with your ability to hold that string back. With the 'fingers' pad, you'll be able to hold that string until you're ready to let it go, which is definitely important when you're doing anything. Even shooting for fun you want to make sure that you have the right hold on the string so you don't let go before you're ready and mess up your score.

Arm Guard: A lot of people tend to have problems with twisting their bow a little when they let it go. When the string releases it releases a whole lot of pent-up energy. That energy can cause the back of the bow to twist around and the string to hit your arm. If you hold your bow with your wrist slightly bent (which you shouldn't but sometimes it happens) you could also release the string directly into your arm. The space on the inside of your non-dominant hand is where you'll find the most problems because that's the hand you're going to use to hold the bow.

An arm guard is a piece of plastic (usually) that may be coated with fabric. It then has elastic straps on it that help keep it firmly against your forearm. If you don't wear one you might find yourself with some welts and red marks on the inside of your arm, at least until you figure out how to hold the bow straight and keep it straight after you've released the arrow. It's definitely a good thing to have when you're first starting out, and the good thing is that it doesn't cost much in order to get it. They're actually quite inexpensive to find (or even make your own).

Eye Patch: If you're not able to close one eye you're going to want an eye patch to help you out. When you're shooting, you're going to use your dominant eye, which may or may not be the same as your dominant hand. The other eye you need to be able to close so you aren't getting mixed messages as you're trying to line up the shot. If you're able to close one eye then you're going to be off and running, but not everyone is able to do that easily, and that means you may need a little bit of assistance to keep you going. An eye patch is a great way to help you until you can train yourself to close that one eye.

Arrows: You're not going to get very far without having some arrows to put in your bow. Your arrows can be made with many different types of material but the best are usually made with carbon fiber. This is very lightweight and easy to use and it's also less prone to breaking or bending. They can be a bit expensive, however, so it's important to keep that in mind before you go to purchase arrows. You could end up spending a lot of money on them and you want at least 6-8.

Another aspect of your arrows to keep in mind is what's going to make them fly. Arrows have what is called fletching on them. That fletching is the pieces at the end. Arrows will typically have three of these 'feathers' but what they are made of and the form they take will differ between different types. Some people prefer solid, plastic fletching. These are less prone to breaking if you shoot arrows close together but they don't tend to fly quite as well.

The other option is actually feathers. Now, they're not real feathers like the ones that come from a bird, but they're made with small pieces of material glued together to get you as close to a feather as you can get. They fly straighter and smoother, but if you shoot too close together you'll knock some of the pieces out and have to replace your feathers sooner.

Chapter III

Understanding Your Compound Bow

If you've never shot in your life you probably don't really know about the different types of bows, right? Don't feel bad. Most people don't. But a compound is one of the simplest types of bows to shoot. It may not seem that way since it has a lot more pieces to it, but it's actually going to require a little less from you. Of course, some people believe that a compound bow also requires less strength and less skill, so it's going to be up to you what you think and what you'd rather do.

A compound bow is always made by a machine. That's because they are always made out of composite materials or things like aluminum, magnesium alloy or carbon fiber. Each of these materials is going to make the bow durable and strong without making it heavy at the same time. After all, you could easily have to hold that bow up for a long period of time before you make the shot and let it down. If it's too heavy you're not going to be able to do that and that's definitely not going to help in a competition or when you're trying to hunt for food.

A compound bow isn't going to have a single curved shape to it like the bows you've probably always seen in pictures. Instead, it has limbs on each end (top and bottom) that curve towards the center, but then there will be some alternative shapes in between. This is where you'll see the sights, the arrow rest and (if you have them) the stabilizer and wrist strap. On the opposite side you'll see the string that connects the ends of the limbs, but on the ends of them are what's called cams.

The strings run over the cams and they help make the bow easier to pull back. After all, that compound bow would take a whole lot of effort to pull back if you had to do it all by hand. The cams help take away some of that weight. On the string, you may have little stringy pieces that help to keep the bow quiet, a round piece of plastic that is wrapped into the string and small knobs that help you figure out where to knock the arrow and where to attach your release. All of this makes it a whole lot easier for you to shoot the bow and see what you're aiming at.

When you're ready to shoot you put your hand through the wrist strap to grab the ergonomic grip. You clip the knock (the little plastic piece at the back of the arrow) over the string. It's usually going to clip between two small pieces of rubber and it will make a clicking sound when it's latched. Set the other side of the arrow on top of the arrow rest, all the way across the bow. Clip your release below the arrow (it will have a specified area as well) and pull it back slowly. Once you do, you want to pull it up so the fingers on the release are right next to your cheek.

You should be able to see through the round piece of plastic, called a peep sight, and straight through to the sight on the other side. You line up the sights with where you want to shoot and you slowly squeeze the lever on the release to shoot your arrow. It's a long process, but all of the moving pieces definitely make it a whole lot easier for you to actually get the shot that you're looking for. If you're looking for something more traditional, however, you'll want to check out what you can do with a recurve. These are closer to the bows that our ancestors would have used, and they have a lot less moving parts.

Chapter IV

Understanding Your Recurve

If you're looking at getting into archery but you're interested in a more traditional approach you may want to look at a recurve. These bows are about the same size as a compound bow, but that's where the similarities end (at least for the most part). With a recurve, you'll notice the end actually curves out rather than forming a rounded surface. What you end up with is a curve in the middle that curves back a little as it reaches the endpoints.

The ends are turned out, but the string still attaches on both sides and creates a space to knock your arrow and to attach a release (if you're using one). These types of bows can be made out of a number of different materials. They may be made with the same aluminum or composite materials that a compound is or they may even be made out of wood. That's because some people (keeping with the more traditional theme) like to make their own bow instead of purchasing one. Keep in mind, this is going to be a long and difficult process, but for some people, it's absolutely worth it. Only you can tell if it's worth it for you.

When you look at this type of bow you'll generally only see the material that the curved portion is made of and the string that holds it all together. That's because a lot of people who use a recurve are going to be more traditionalist and don't want to spoil it by adding a whole bunch of other pieces (like those we talked about with the compound bow). Of course, some people who use a recurve will still add some other pieces to it so shooting is a little bit easier.

For the most part, you're going to see a very limited number of accessories on a recurve bow. One of those may be an arrow rest, that provides an easier place to set the arrow when it's attached to the string. Some recurves have a slightly carved out area that the arrow fits into rather than having to add a separate piece as well, but that's going to be up to you and whoever is in charge of making the bow (or where you purchase it from). This carved area is slightly more traditional than adding a piece as well.

You may also find some recurve bows with sights on them. These are less traditional because a lot of more traditional users believe they should try to hit the target based on their own ability without that added tool. This usually means finding a specific point on the bow itself that serves as a good sight rather than having an accessory that will help you out. It's definitely going to be more complicated that way, but you'll have a more traditional experience and for some people, that's the most important thing (or the most fun one).

On the other side of things, you may or may not use a release if you're using a recurve bow. Some people still like the idea of a release because it makes holding the string back a little easier and also makes it smoother to let go. Others think it takes away from the traditional aspect and they may choose to use fingers. Now, you can opt to use your fingers directly on the string, but this can be a little difficult and a little painful. You have to be able to keep your fingers flat, instead of hooked around the string, because pulling your fingers away when they're hooked can cause the bow to bounce a little.

If you aren't able to do this, or you don't want to risk hurting your fingers, you may want to get 'fingers.' These little pads usually hook over your middle finger and provide a softer and smoother surface that you can hook around the string. When you want to release it you can easily slide your fingers (and the pad) off the string, without having to worry about jerking it. And you can also hold it back longer without having to worry about hurting your fingers.

When you're ready to shoot you clip the arrow onto the string, set the other end on the arrow rest and hook your release or fingers around the string. The release hooks under the arrow or your fingers go around the nock of the arrow. Then you pull back the string and bring your hand up so the side of it hits your cheek, just like with a compound bow. You sight in either with sights or with whatever spot you've found to help you and you release the lever on the release or slide your fingers off the string to release. It definitely makes things simpler, but hitting the target in the right place is definitely more difficult.

Chapter V

The Target Options for Your Practice

So you've figured out which bow you think you want to shoot. You have the equipment you need and the accessories for your bow. Now you're trying to figure out what you should be shooting at, right? You've already decided that you need to practice before you go hunting (or maybe that hunting isn't the right experience for you at all). So now it's time to head to a range or to your own backyard and start figuring out how that bow really works.

The first thing is figuring out types of targets. There are actually quite a few different options that you can try out and each one is going to give you a slightly different experience. The best thing, however, is that you can easily switch back and forth between different target options whenever you want. Just because you start out with one thing doesn't mean you always have to shoot the same thing. In fact, it's definitely recommended that you try out plenty of other things.

The simplest targets that you can shoot are the ones you probably think of when we first talk about archery targets. These are the round ones that have circles that get progressively smaller as they go in. You get a yellow ring at the center and other colors including red, blue, white and black around. These targets are not only the most common when it comes to target practice, but they're also some of the easiest to start out with because you can easily see where you want to hit.

The closer to the center of a target you're able to get the better you're doing. With these larger targets, you have a larger area to aim at and that definitely helps in your practice. When you start looking at other targets you're going to have smaller areas that you want to hit, and that means you need to be a better shot before you'll be able to get a good score. With this type of target, you're going to get 5 points for every arrow in the yellow (at the very center). You get 4 points for everything in the red (the next circle out), 3 for everything in the blue, 2 for black and 1 for white. Anything outside the white ring gets 0 points.

When you start looking at more advanced targets you may see one that looks very similar but in smaller targets. These have three small targets to a sheet instead of one large one, and they're missing the outer two colors of rings. These are another type of target archery option and they are scored the same way, but without those two outer rings. You also have to be able to hit each target at least once in order to get points (at least if you're in any type of league you do). But of course, if you're just practicing these help you get an idea of aiming at different areas and smaller targets.

Another type of target is black and white and has five targets on it. This one will only have a white center and a black outer ring. These can also help you figure out how to get a smaller and smaller area and without the benefit of the bright color to help you. You get 5 points for anything in the white section inside and 4 points for anything in the black (or possibly blue) section on the outside. Anything outside those areas doesn't get you any points at all. These can be good when you're working on shrinking your sighting area or when you're trying to get a better handle on sighting in quickly in certain areas.

Of course, if you're just looking to practice you'll find tons of paper targets available just about anywhere. You'll find animal targets (the paper kind), tic tac toe boards, unique shapes and pictures and just about anything you could possibly imagine. That's because, when you're shooting paper targets (unless it's for competition) it's mostly about having fun, so there are all kinds of different options available to choose from.

Each target is going to have a different scoring mechanism (since that's how you know if you did good or not) but it's entirely up to you if you decide to actually use those scoring options or if you just decide to have some fun and shoot at them. The great thing about targets is that they're not very expensive, so you can easily buy a whole bundle of them and use them with friends. Plus, you can use them as long as you want because you score before you pull the arrows out, so you always know which arrows actually made which holes.

Chapter VI

Indoor Target Archery

So let's say you've decided you want to start shooting and you have everything you need, including the targets, the bow, the accessories and everything else. So now you have to decide where you actually want to shoot. One of the options is to take all of your equipment indoors and start practicing this sport somewhere nice and warm (though if you already live in a nice, warm area that may be a moot point). Indoor archery spaces can be fun and you may even find groups and leagues that you can join while you're at it.

Indoor ranges are available at a lot of different archery clubs or even some gun clubs. You want to take a look in your area and see what they have and find out what they have to offer for people who aren't members. After all, you don't want to become a member when you're not sure you're really going to like the sport, right? You want to give it a chance before you start jumping into anything in particular and that's easy enough to do at most clubs. Just make sure you find out about their visitor policies.

An indoor range should be large enough that you can practice reasonably well. While your bow will be able to shoot at 7 or 10 yards (or even less) you'll want something that has at least a little more than that. As long as you can shoot 20 to 30 yards you'll be able to get some good practice in and really get an idea for the sport. Shooting up close is okay, but it's even more fun when you can get further away from the target and get something really great. It feels a whole lot more exciting (and it takes more skill).

An indoor range needs to be built so that you can shoot without being too close to other people. After all, that arrow you're shooting is going to be traveling at an extremely high rate of speed and it's super sharp at the end (even though when you poke your finger with it you may not notice). You need to make sure you're following all of the safety precautions. We'll lay out most of them later on with some of the tips and tricks, but keeping the arrows away from anyone and everyone is going to be the most important step.

When you are looking at a range make sure you pay attention to how it's set up and the safety features they tell you about. The shooting room for an indoor range should have an entrance located at the back. That means when you're shooting no one should be popping up down at the end where your target is located. If someone enters the room at any point during shooting they should be behind you, so there's never any danger that they are going to be hit by a stray arrow or that someone will unintentionally shoot in their direction (which could happen if they walk into the room from the other end).

It's best if the room you're shooting in isn't directly the one you walk into from outdoors either. Think about it, if you're shooting at a target and all the sudden you get hit with a blast of cold air or warm air or just plain wind, it's going to throw you off, right? That's definitely not going to be fun. Plus, if people are walking in and out of that room all the time it's going to be difficult to keep it at a comfortable temperature for shooting.

Different clubhouses and indoor ranges are going to be set up in different ways, but checking out a few different ones to see how they are set up and what they can offer you is definitely going to be a benefit. You'll be able to see what you like and what you don't and you'll be able to pick and choose where you feel more comfortable shooting (or where you're going to get the greatest features). Then you can choose where (and if) you want to become an actual member.

Chapter VII

Outdoor Target Archery

Okay, so you've decided that you're going to start shooting archery and you've got all the equipment that you need. And maybe you've tried out shooting indoors or maybe you don't really think that's going to be the ideal option for you. So what do you do next? What's your other option? Well, the next option is to head outdoors and take all of your equipment with you. No, don't worry, we're not going to be hunting at this point. You're still going to be shooting targets, but you're going to be doing it outdoors instead of indoors.

The great thing about shooting outside is that you get to experience the fresh air. It's going to be healthier for you just because of that and you may even have more fun because it feels a little more realistic. Even if you're not shooting at actual animals (or even animal targets) you get to have a similar experience to hunting. For some people, this is the best option because you get the good parts of the hunting experience without actually killing anything (which a lot of people don't really like). So why not give it a try and see what happens?

Just like with an indoor range you can get a lot of different lengths to choose from when it comes to outdoor archery. The nice thing about being outdoors, however, is that the targets are easier to move. Instead of having one single line where everyone stands to shoot from and everyone shoots at the same distance, an outdoor range offers more options. Often you'll find targets that are set up at different distances so even though the line you shoot from is the same, the line you're shooting to is going to be different. This can be great for more advanced shooters who are shooting next to beginners.

The same as will indoor ranges, however, you can shoot at any type of paper target you may want. Some outdoor ranges even have what are called 3-D targets, which are actually animals or other structures made out of foam and composite materials that you can shoot at. Otherwise, the paper target is usually affixed to a hay bale to make it easy to shoot without having to worry about the arrow going through or getting too stuck when you're trying to pull it back out for your next shoot.

An outdoor range should have the same type of setup that an indoor range does, however. It should always be facing away from people and into an area that could not pose a danger. If you miss the target entirely and shoot over or to the side, where is your arrow going to go? The answer should be a hill or some other soft surface that will absorb the impact. You should never be shooting towards a parking lot, homes or any area where there could be children or adults. You want the arrows to be going somewhere safe, no matter if you hit where you're aiming or not.

You also want to make sure that no one is going to sneak up on you at the opposite end of the range. That doesn't mean that it needs to be closed in (though some are) but it does need to be blocked off so no one is going to get too close to the sides of the range. If your arrow goes off the side it could hurt someone that way and no one wants that to happen. You want to make sure people are always walking up behind you when you are shooting instead of in front.

One nice thing about these outdoor ranges, however, is that you can easily see people coming up toward you from the sides, which can keep you and everyone else safer. You know if they are getting too close so you can stop shooting. It's important to remember that if anyone is in front of you, even a little bit, while you're shooting, you should stop. You don't want to risk a wayward arrow that could easily put someone in a lot of danger. After all, there's no telling what could happen to an arrow after you let it go.

Chapter VIII

Competing in Target Archery

Okay, so you've picked up the equipment and given target archery a shot. Now you're thinking you might want to get a little more serious about it, right? Well, it's definitely possible. Competitive archery isn't as well known a sport as, say, football, but there are definitely plenty of people who are doing it and you shouldn't discount this as a super fun pastime if you're interested in archery yourself. After all, what could be better than spending time doing something you enjoy?

The great thing about competition in archery is that you get a whole lot of freedom about how you want to compete and where you want to compete. If you're just getting started you can definitely check out clubs and leagues. These will give you a more comfortable and relaxed setting to start competing. After all, if you're not really sure what you're doing you don't want to shell out a lot of money on entrance fees for a competition that you're not really sure how to go about it, right? That's why you want to look at places you can get started first.

Most areas have at least a couple clubs, whether they're small or large may depend on how big your town or city is. Which style you feel more comfortable at will depend entirely on you. But your best option, when you think you may want to start competing, is to look at joining a club and being part of a league. These types of leagues usually have less than 30 people involved and you all meet once a week to shoot at a specific type of targets.

With club leagues, you may find several options like animal leagues, 20-yard leagues, and even traditional style leagues.

All of these options let you pick what you're most comfortable with and go from there. Once you've decided the type of targets and the distances you feel comfortable shooting at you can join the league and see how you do. Most leagues are only going to last a set number of weeks and then you'll see who wins. It's fun and it's a way to meet other people who are interested in archery too, but if you're looking to get anything out of it other than perhaps a plaque or a trophy you're not going to find that in a standard league.

For those who want to get really involved in competitions, you'll want to check out the Archery Shooters Association and the National Field Archery Association, which always have competitions going on. Those competitions take place throughout the country and even in different parts of the world. What's even better is there are all different kinds of competitions with different standards, different rules, and different classifications. So you can always find something that will work for you and whatever level you're currently at. That's important so you don't get into the wrong group of people far more advanced and get discouraged.

Archery competitions are generally going to be quite specialized. They require you to shoot from a certain distance and even to use a certain type of bow. They'll also require you to shoot at a specific type of target. All of this is to ensure everyone has an equal chance and that the standards are the same for each person. If you think you're ready for one of these competitions it's best to check the websites for each of the top organizations already mentioned. They'll help you find the right competition for you based on your shooting abilities and what you're looking for, as well as things like entrance fees, locations and a whole lot more.

When you do start competing make sure you give it a few chances and see what you think. One competition may not be the right fit for you, but if you try out a few different types of competition you may find something that really works or helps you do better. After all, not everyone is good at one thing or there wouldn't be different kinds of competition. Make sure you're also not jumping in too fast. Trying to compete without a lot of practice is definitely not going to keep you feeling good about your skills.

Chapter IX

Tips and Tricks Your Coach Will Tell You

If you're just getting started or you're not entirely sure that you want to start archery you may not want to get a coach to teach you. Having a coach can be expensive, at least, if you're getting a private one. That means you want to know that you're into the sport before you want to pay someone to really help you get good. But how do you get to where you can enjoy it without that coach in the first place? It's not as bad as you might think. You just have to know some of the tips and tricks that go along with things.

- Your dominant hand is not always your dominant eye. What that means is, just because you write with your right-hand doesn't mean that your right eye is the dominant one. You need to know your dominant eye before you can get the right kind of bow.

- One easy way to figure out your dominant eye is by using an object in the room with you. Point to something across the room like you are trying to show it to someone. Now, holding your finger out, close your left eye. Does your finger appear to move? If it doesn't you are right eye dominant. If it does close your right eye. Does your finger appear to move now? If it doesn't you are left eye dominant. This tells you which arm should hold the bow and which eye to close when you're sighting in.

- If you are right eye dominant you will stand with your left side facing the target and your left foot closer to the target. You will hold the bow in your left hand and pull back the string with your right.

- If you are left eye dominant you will stand with your right side facing the target and your right foot closer to the target. You will hold the bow in your right hand and pull back the string with your left.

- Keep in mind that most people are right eye dominant just like most people are right-handed. It doesn't mean there's anything wrong with being left eye dominant, it simply means if you stand in a row of people shooting at the same time you will likely be facing the opposite direction as them.

- Just because you are right-handed does not mean you are right eye dominant or vice versa (though it usually will happen that way).

- Always stand with your feet perpendicular to the target. Put your front foot on the line of where you're shooting from (10-yard line, 20-yard line, etc.) then put your back foot about shoulder width away. Make sure your feet are lined up so your toes are in line with each other and your heels are in line. Now slide your back foot forward just a little so that there's a slight angle between the toes on your front foot and the toes on your back foot. This is your basic stance.

- Keep your feet steady and don't let them move while you shoot.

- Keep your shoulders and back straight while you're pulling the string back, holding it and letting it go.

- Squeeze your finger on the trigger without jerking. If you jerk your finger down on the trigger you'll end up throwing off your shot by jerking the string as well.

- Once you squeeze the trigger hold still until you hear the arrow hit the wall (or the target). This is called follow-through and if you don't follow through you'll end up twisting your bow and spinning your arrow off in the wrong direction (at least slightly).

- Never step in front of the shooting line while anyone else is shooting or if they have an arrow on their bow.

- Never put an arrow on your bow or even take it out of the quiver when someone is ahead of the shooting line.

- Do not release your string without an arrow on it. This can actually cause damage to the bow because the pent-up energy and power from pulling back the string has nowhere to go but back into the bow.

Chapter X

Is Target Archery For You?

So it is for you? Are you interested in becoming an archer or a hunter? Are you thinking about picking up a bow and arrows and some equipment so you can see what it's really all about? Maybe this book has made you think about it, but maybe you're still not sure this is where you want to be or what you want to be doing. So let's check it out.

Do you like the idea of hunting for your own food? If you think it would be really cool to be out there hunting for food for your family and getting your own meat then it might be a great opportunity for you to get started. Target archery is going to allow you to experience what it's like to hunt before you get out there and actually start shooting animals for your food. It's also a good way to practice between seasons.

Are you looking for a winter sport to participate in? A lot of leagues run through the winter months because hunters aren't out in the woods during that time. You might find some casual events through the summer as well. All of this together is going to give you something to do during seasons that you might be looking for just that. It lets you head inside for some sports even during the colder parts of the year or head outside and enjoy yourself when the weather starts getting a little bit nicer, which is definitely a bonus.

Do you like competitive sports? If you do then archery is a great sport to get involved with because it has just the right mix of competition and just plain fun. You get to have some fun with other people and if you join a league it's going to be even more good-natured competition instead of getting too competitive. Of course, if you want to be really competitive it's easy enough to do that as well because there are always events and tournaments going on somewhere in the country or even in all areas abroad.

Are you looking for a reason to travel? If you want to get involved in competitive archery you'll definitely have plenty of reason to travel because there are competitions going on throughout all parts of the country and the world. You'll be able to pick where you want to go and find a competition just about anywhere at just about any time of the year. It can definitely be a great experience for you and it's something you'll be able to enjoy with family as well because you can always take them with you on your next trips whenever you want to go.

Do you want an activity the whole family can do together? Archery is great for kids of all ages and adults. There are specialty equipment options when you're looking for someone really small, but they'll still be able to have fun with the sport. Plus adults can pick it up in no time as well. That's definitely a great opportunity because everyone in your family can get involved together and can even learn together. Why not take that initiative and see what you can all learn? Archery may be a little more expensive with more people, but it's going to be more fun too.

Are you looking for an inexpensive sports option? Archery can get expensive if you want to buy the best of the best equipment or if you decide to get really into it, but when you're just starting out it doesn't have to be that bad. There are plenty of places you can get cheaper or secondhand equipment that will help you get an idea for what you like or don't like. Plus, consider how much it costs to get involved in most other sports. Archery is definitely not going to seem that bad when you think about soccer, baseball and all those other things you could be doing and what you need to play.

Are you trying to get in shape? If so, archery is a great way to do it. You're going to be using your core a whole lot and definitely your arms in order to pull back that bow and hold it back for an extended period of time. You'll also need to pull it back repeatedly, which is going to be a great, and continuous, workout for your arms. So you'll actually be able to keep toning your entire body as you keep shooting.

Have you ever wanted to be Robin Hood? Or Katniss Everdeen? Or Hawkeye? If you've ever wanted to be any of these fun heroes or even any others, you'll definitely want to see what all the fuss is about, right? Come on, there's got to be a reason that these people chose to use a bow and arrow as their weapon of choice, right? There is. It's a really cool piece of equipment and it lets you really focus on what you're doing. It takes some practice, but you can definitely see what it is about this sport that all of them love.

Maybe one (or more) of these things sounds like you. Maybe none of them sounds like you. But no matter what, you're going to find archery to be a great experience. Even if you decide you don't like to do it extensively or you don't even want to do it again, it will be something interesting and unique that you can try out. If you decide you like it you'll have a blast checking out clubs and leagues and even competitions and getting your entire family involved. If you don't ... well, it will be something really cool that you can tell your kids and the rest of your family that you tried, right?

Conclusion

Hopefully, with the help of this book, you've learned a little something about target archery and how it can be useful for you. Maybe you've learned how to get started or what you should be doing to pick out some of the best equipment. Maybe you're interested in joining a club now or searching for the best store where you can pick up your equipment. Maybe you're even thinking about going out hunting once you get a chance to practice a bit more.

No matter what you're planning to do with this knowledge, hopefully, it's been an informative experience and a little bit of fun. Make sure you at least take a little time to head to your nearest outdoors or hunting store so you can try out shooting a bow. You might just be hooked on it before you even know it. It can even be something that you enjoy with the rest of your family if you want to get them into the sport as well.

Keep in mind, this isn't going to be one of the least expensive sports you can get involved in, but it's definitely going to be one that you can get even young children and older people involved in. That means you can all have some fun with it together. Having activities to do as a family can be great, so make sure you give target archery a shot. It can become an amazing experience and it will most definitely be something unique.

Target archery begins and ends with you. If you're looking for a once in a while hobby there's no reason not to give target archery a shot. If you're looking for something that you can really get involved with and take through the competitive level ... well then you're definitely going to have no reason not to choose target archery as the way to do it. Whether you want to give hunting a shot or not, you're going to have a blast with archery to get you started on trying something different.

We wish you all the best on your travels and on your experience with target archery. Hopefully, you'll find it just as enjoyable as all the other people who continue to join the sport every single day. If not ... well, what do you have to lose by trying something new? You'll at least have a whole new skill and time spent with your family.

Win a free

kindle
OASIS

Let us know what you thought of this book to enter the sweepstake at:

http://booksfor.review/archery

Made in United States
Orlando, FL
21 December 2023